Withdrawn from
Davidson College Library

Library of
Davidson College

The EDUCATION of the PUBLIC

MALCOLM L. WARFORD

The Education of the Public

by Malcolm L. Warford

The Pilgrim Press
New York, Philadelphia

Copyright © 1980 The Pilgrim Press
All rights reserved

No part of this publication may be reproduced, stored in a retrieval system, or transmitted in any form or by any means, electronic, mechanical, photocopying, recording, or otherwise (brief quotations used in magazines or newspaper reviews excepted), without the prior permission of the publisher.

Library of Congress Cataloging in Publication Data
Warford, Malcolm L. 1942-
   The education of the public.

   (The Education of the public and the public school)
   1. Public schools—United States. I. Title. II. Series: Education of the public and the public school.
LA217.W36   371'.01'0973   80-21336
ISBN 0-8298-0418-8

The Pilgrim Press, 132 W. 31 Street, New York, New York 10001

Introduction

"Education in the schools as well as education in the home, church and community is under critical examination. To meet the urgent needs of all persons, especially those of children and youth, the church is called to the renewal of a long standing commitment to secure for each child of God that education which will fully develop his or her capacities and which will enable that person to serve as a responsible person in the common life. This commitment is based on our belief that there are coherent patterns of purpose and meaning in human life to which education must point if it is to assist humankind in the pursuit of truth and the fulfillment of human destiny. Participation in efforts to improve education is a continuing moral responsibility for every Christian." (From "The Church and the Public School," a position paper of the United Church Board for Homeland Ministries, May, 1979)

The public school is not lacking for doomsayers or critics; they are as abundant as the locusts and frogs of the plagues of Egypt. Nor is the public school lacking in moral cheerleaders who have their own righteous demands of what the school is to be and to do; they are as abundant as the tongues of Babel. There is no abundance, however, of persons and groups who perceive what is at stake for all of the people of the republic and for the republic itself in the present crisis in the public school and who accept their public responsibility for the welfare of the public school.

The monograph series is issued not as a directive from the church to the public school but as an aid to persons in the churches and the public at large who care about the public school and who, with others in their communities, seek a basis for understanding and addressing some of the complex problems of their public schools.

The monographs are published by the United Church Board for Homeland Ministries whose own tradition of commitment to the education of the public reaches back to the settlement of the nation and whose tradition of commitment to the public school extends to its formation in seventeenth century New England. This tradition respects and advocates the distinctiveness of the role of the church and the school but it also recognizes their common responsibility for the welfare of persons and the society. We hope these monographs strengthen that common commitment.

Members of the Public Education Issue Group which developed the monographs include Percel O. Alston, Robert A. Mayo, Audrey Miller and Verlyn Barker, Chairperson, from the staff of United Church Board for Homeland Ministries, and Harold Viehman, staff, United Ministries in Education. Douglas Sloan, Professor of History and Education and Editor of the *Teachers College Record,* Teachers College, Columbia University, served as an invaluable Consultant to the Issue Group.

Verlyn L. Barker

Oneself exists by virtue of a world shared with other selves. Our life is the intersection of the Self with an Other. In the intense personal form this intersection is love, and in the ideal, general form it's the Republic.[1]

Ross Lockridge, Jr.

Everyone knows what the public is until asked to define it. I want to suggest that the public refers to a people, and, in this case, to the American people and our sense of a shared history and purpose. The public is formed by our ways of being with one another. It is sustained by language, symbols and events that interpret the significance of our common life. While the public ultimately relates to the whole inhabited earth (the *oikoumene*), we participate in this universal public only as we are able to commit ourselves to the part of the public that is ours by inheritance or by adoption. At the heart of the public is a set of personal, social and economic relationships that exist between ourselves and others. In this regard citizenship is nothing less than the way we care for these relationships.[2]

Our sense of the public is greater than the shape of the society at any given time. We should recognize that the American ideal sometimes has been a shallow hope as various Americans have been excluded from consideration as equals in the promise of the Republic. The sad history of separation of black and white into unequal camps of dignity and opportunity has been the shadow side of our more exhuberant protestations of public good. Too often the Republic has ignored the shape of tragedy and excised from public view the scenes of suffering, discrimination and economic inequity that have been the lot of many Americans. Moreover, in seeking national interests we have sometimes suspended our responsibilities to the whole human community in pursuit of a seemingly manifest, yet elusive destiny.

In our best moments as a people, however, we have understood that our commitments as citizens of this nation are most appropriately expressed as we are aware of our concommitant responsibilities to the rest of the people on the earth. Consider in this respect the words of an elder of the Oglala Sioux who reported a vision of this universal public: "I saw that the sacred hoop of my people was one of many hoops that made one circle, wide as daylight and as starlight, and in the center grew one mighty flowering tree to shelter all the children of one mother and father. And I saw that it was holy."[3] In a similar vein, but from an entirely different kind of American, Benjamin Franklin once prayed that God would "grant, that not only the Love of Liberty, but a thorough Knowledge of the Rights of Man, may pervade all the Nations of the Earth, so that a Philosopher may set his Foot anywhere on its Surface, and say, 'This is My Country.'"[4]

The Education of the Public

To speak of the education of the public is to direct attention to the various means by which a people sustain their common values, beliefs and behaviors. Within this context, our identification of public education with schooling alone is an indiscriminate use of the terms. They are not the same. Schooling is only one agency in the configuration of agencies that collectively educate the public. Families, political parties, television networks, museums, the armed services, social clubs and voluntary associations of all kinds together participate in the education of the attitudes and perceptions that shape our private hopes and our public expectations. All of these various agencies should help inform us of our ties to one another, the rest of the world and our place in it.

This does not suggest, though, that one can reduce public education to some list of uniquely American virtues that should be inculcated through formal instruction. Whenever the sense of being an American has been simplified in this way, it has ended up as one group's inflation of its own lore to mythical proportions. Contrary to this, I think the public exists only to the extent that we are able to sustain the vitality of many small publics that mediate our differences and support a series of mutual relationships that express the richness of our diversity. The nation is founded on the idea that such diversity is the greatest gift a people may possess. If we reject this notion and view public education as training in consensus then we search for sameness. Such a search becomes socially coercive and destructive. The public as an ideal is best represented in the promise of a democratic society composed of many different people and communities united by a common hope that expressed traditionally says that this nation is a government of, by and for people conceived in liberty and dedicated to the proposition that all of humanity is created equal.

The Crisis of the Public

Throughout American society there is a vague but nonetheless real feeling that the public is in crisis. The most immediate signs of this crisis are expressed in the technocratic and increasingly impersonal character of society, the emergence of seemingly unmanageable energy and economic problems, the failure of schools to educate the young, and the erosion of the communities and neighborhoods that once sustained the value and ties of our common life.

The crisis of the public is reflected especially in issues related to public schooling. For example, lack of adequate funding has caused school districts to close their schools temporarily. Controversy over busing has polarized communities where courts have intervened to settle educational questions that have appeared to be insoluble on the local level. In other places, textbooks have been at the center of disputes among various citizen groups who disagree on the content of the books adopted for the classroom. Teacher strikes have become regular occasions on the national scene as financial retrenchments have led to the dismissal of some staff and only modest salary increments for others. And, a general feeling of skepticism toward public schools seems to be growing as parents in various parts of the country question the quality of instruction.

Too often we have viewed the crises of schooling apart from the more fundamental problem of the public itself. In so doing, we have lost sight of the deeper educational problems reflected in schooling issues. In this essay, I want to define the nature of public education, examine in broad outline the history of education and schooling that has brought us to the current moment, and then isolate some key issues that need to be raised as we situate the crises of schooling within the more systemic problem of the public's education.

Education as the Formation of the Public

The origins of American public education can be traced to our ancestors' hope that a new republic might be established on this continent and a new people formed. We are indebted particularly to two major cultural traditions that have provided the foundation for our understanding of how this public was to be educated: the classical tradition of the Greeks and Romans and the faith and life of the Jewish people. It is important, therefore, that we look at some essential Greco-Roman ideas concerning the education of the public (*res publica*) and Hebraic traditions regarding the formation of the people of God.

The Classical Tradition

The classical education tradition in western civilization has been centered in the formation of the individual within an image of the public good. The Greek and Roman conception of the educated person was the citizen. In this sense, education was the process of induction into the *polis,* or city-state. All the various experiences of everyday life were perceived as occasions when the ideal of the culture could be communicated. The formal occasions of schooling were relatively rare, essentially confined to an elite. Yet all of life, from family life to the athletic games to the affairs of state, were seen as parts of a configuration of learning. Education, then, was the process by which the community formed the individual. It was the conscious effort of a society to pass on its values and understandings of what it means to be human.

The Greeks used the term *paideia* to refer to both the ideal and the process by which the life of each citizen could be nurtured by the ultimate values of the community. Werner Jaeger identified four basic characteristics of this *paideia*: 1) the value of the individual; 2) the importance of the arts in all the affairs of life; 3) a concern with the universal in human reality; and 4) the intrinsic relationship between ideas, the affairs of state, and the development of individual character. This conscious ideal of the public was not a lofty pattern existing in the realm of speculation.[5] For the Greeks, the preparation of individuals for participation in the affairs of the community was the goal and the rationale of education. Indeed, one of the salient characteristics of Greek *paideia* was the importance of addressing the nature of the public, testing its strength and trying to move the society to wrestle with its problems.

At different times in the history of western civilization, the classical tradition has been rediscovered and emulated. In particular, the Renaissance was a time in which the ideals of Greece and Rome were celebrated with particular vigor. But in the rediscovery, there was an adaptation made of that tradition. More and more, the classical tradition came to be regarded as an intellectual tradition concerned primarily with arts, letters and modes of civility. In its most extreme form, the emulation of ancient classical culture simply became another elitist exercise in fine manners. In our own day, the classical tradition transposed into the postures of modern humanism hinges upon the individual's attempts to be authentic. It tends to sever the connection between the individual and the community as the person seeks to express a particular inner truth. In this sense, the classical tradition becomes identified with forms of romantic self-expression that bear little relationship to Greek ideals of education. In ancient culture, it was not possible to envision the individual apart from the community itself. The definitions of virtue, truth, beauty and goodness were all derived from the life of the mind in the community, and not apart from it. The essential educational question for the Greeks was ultimately a political question, the nature of the public life.

The Hebraic Tradition in Education

In Israel, education was focused on instruction in the Torah. Yahweh was seen as the ultimate teacher and the Torah (the law as a way of life) was perceived as the source of knowledge. Family life was both the setting and the mode of instruction. While royalty were tutored, and scribes, priests and Levites did receive training in their particular roles, there were no formal systems of schooling other than the rituals, observances and practices of the family and its extensions in the society.

In another sense, however, the entire community of Israel was the primary educator. The great cultic occasions in the nation's life were celebrations that retold the history of the people, lifted up the major themes of faith, and provided an event whereby the covenant was renewed and the reality of God reaffirmed. In the spring, for example, the Passover was held at the beginning of the barley harvest to remember the Exodus from Egypt. Pentecost occurred in June during another harvest and was connected with the giving of the law on Sinai. A third major festival was held in September at the end of the grape harvest; it was a cultic remembering of the journey in the desert on the way to the Promised Land. These communal occasions were structured by rituals that retold the stories of faith. The interpretation of faith was the specific responsibility of parents toward their children.

> And these words which I command you this day shall be upon your heart; and you shall teach them diligently to your children, and shall talk of them when you sit in your house, and when you walk by the way, and when you lie down, and when you rise. And you shall bind them as a sign upon your hand, and they shall be as frontlets between your eyes. And you shall write them on the doorposts of your house and on your gates. (Deuteronomy 6:6-9, RSV)

Thus, parental instruction was a religious obligation. Israel's responsibility for proclaiming its faith to the nation was matched by an equivalent demand by Yahweh that families explain the nature of faith and initiate the young into the life of the community. The heart of education, then, in Israel was the understanding of revelation. The explication of the Torah and the stories of the past were told in order that children could understand the acts of God in the history of the people. The Torah, in this sense, should not be seen as a hardened set of legal instructions, but a way of walking before God in the present time. Education, therefore, was aimed at forming the child's understanding of the world, the nature of Yahweh's special relationship to the people of Israel, and the individual's responsibility in the life of the community.

Following the defeat of the nation and the exile in Babylon (586 BC), synagogues and later schools were created in the Jewish communities of the dispersion in order to preserve and to pass on the faith of Israel. At first synagogues were established as centers where the traditions of faith were studied and communicated to the adult members of the congregation. Commentaries on the scriptures were developed to elucidate the meaning of faith, and scholars and rabbis devoted their lives to the study and teaching of the Torah. Eventually schools were attached to the synagogues and the school joined the family and the events of worship as the essential educational agencies of the

Jewish people. Education remained unchanged, however, in its devotion to the Torah as both the end and the means of instruction for the people of Yahweh.

Individuals in Community

Both the classical and the Hebraic traditions represented education as essentially public education. They were concerned about the individual's relationship to the community and the importance of education as a means of incorporating youth into society. They saw education as the transmission of values distinctive to their particular culture. In this way, education was understood as socialization. While formal means of education were rare in both traditions, the Greeks and Romans, as well as the Jews, defined education primarily as the effort to form a people and to pass on from generation to generation their society's understanding of the nature of the individual, the community and the world. Learning, therefore, was largely accomplished through participation in the life of the community. Whether we are looking at the way in which the Greek child was brought to adulthood and initiated into the life of the *polis* or the way in which the Jewish child was brought to the Temple and proclaimed a responsible member of the covenant community, the aim and intent of this education was the same—the formation of a public (a people).

Neither the classical nor the Hebraic educational traditions, however, saw education as uncritical indoctrination. Education was perceived as an initiation into the meaning of life. The Greeks' challenge to "know thyself" was met with the Jews' pursuit of the will of God in their lives; one cultivated insight, the other revelation. Education, therefore, was centered in the mystery of life, the elements of awe and wonder that comprise the deepest moments of existence. The myths, symbols and ceremonies of the community re-presented the conceptions of the world that lay at the center of the people's self-understanding, and it was toward these ultimate realities that education was directed. Within both traditions, there were prophetic traditions that appeared in the form of poets and prophets who called the people's attention to the difference between the culture's ideals and its realities. While neither tradition would recognize modern forms of individualism, both the classical and Hebraic traditions valued the rights of the individual in relationship to the laws and customs of the whole society. Although education was primarily viewed as induction, it was also concerned about the cultivation of the individual's particular calling in the society. The prophet's cry is heard in both cultures as a protest against the corruption of the state, its immorality, and its attempts to dehumanize individuals.

Thus, while there were significant differences between the two traditions, it is crucial that we not counterpoint them as polar opposites. This is particularly important when we perceive that Christian culture was largely derived from a synthesis of the classical and Hebraic traditions. The Christian Church developed out of the confrontation of the two cultures. The churches over time have appropriated these two cultural streams in various ways. Indeed, the two traditions are so interwoven into the history of the churches and western civilization that it is practically impossible to separate them. Thus, it is crucial that we appreciate the significance of the two traditions in establishing the foundation for our own understanding of education as the formation of the public and deepen, therefore, our examination of American public education.

Public Education in America

The classical and the Hebraic understandings of public education as synthesized in the experience of western civilization came to America with the earliest colonists. While many nations other than England contributed settlers for the new world, it was the English rather than the Swedes, the Dutch, the French, or the Spanish who established the basic patterns of our national life. English law, language and custom eventually became the predominating tradition against which others were judged. It is especially important to note the educational influence of one segment of the English colonists who made the transit to America, the Puritans, and to trace the history of education, schools and society in subsequent generations.

Puritan Traditions in Education

The Puritans, who by no means represented a numerical majority in New England, much less in the rest of the colonies, still must be considered as the most influential group in shaping

America's idea of itself. In the Puritan commonwealth, education was a serious affair, a matter of the will; it was not left up to the accidents of everyday life, for the continuation of the community depended upon each generation owning the covenant. The Puritan vision of a new world, and themselves as the new Israel, made the transmission of their piety and civility a religious duty. To create this public, to sustain their unique self-understanding as a people, demanded intentional educational strategies. The Puritans brought with them the educational traditions of Renaissance England with its rediscovery of the philosophical, political and esthetic ideals of classical culture. In addition, they carried the special ideas and institutions of the dissenting tradition represented by themselves and the more radical separatist movements.

Lawrence Cremin has summarized briefly the important components of this English *paideia* that was brought from old to new England:

> Insofar as the colonists transplanted the English village community to America, they transplanted an educational configuration of household, church, and school, each standing in relationship to the others and all mediating the educative influence of didactic literature. The configuration taught in different combinations for different orders of the society, the values and substance of piety, civility, and learning.[6]

The church, in particular, stood at the center of the common life of the people; it was the meeting house for public worship and governance as well. While not all colonists belonged to the church, its faith and practice were the matrix that nurtured the life of the society. Puritan society was undifferentiated to the extent that it did not recognize the contemporary division between public and private that we take for granted. The public referred to the society and included an understanding of the self, the community and the world. The Puritans appropriated the Hebraic imagery of the chosen people. They saw America as God's promised land and themselves as the saving remnant that would be a light for all the nations. In educating themselves and their children, the Puritans tried to sustain a view of the world and to communicate a vision of reality that stretched far into the promise of the future and back into the origins of time itself. Their present experience was understood within this wider span of history as part of God's unfolding providence. As early as

1630, Massachusetts' Governor John Winthrop indicated the special character of America and the particular calling of the people who were to settle the land and form the new commonwealth:

> For we must consider that we shall be as a city upon a hill, the eyes of all people are upon us. So that if we shall deal falsely with our God in this work we have undertaken and so cause Him to withdraw His present help from us, we shall be made a story and a byword through the world.[7]

Along with the church, the household was integral to the educational pattern. It was the first source of learning. The family was seen as the "little commonwealth." It was the primary community in which the nature of the larger society was to be understood. The importance of the family as an agency of the public's education is underscored by the various laws that were passed in New England during the 17th century that made it a legal obligation for parents and apprentice masters to provide for the rudimentary education of the young. One of the early concerns of the colonists was the inability of the family to meet all the educational expectations of the community. The Puritans quickly realized that the family by itself could not sustain a new society. The demands of earning a living, building homes and enduring the difficulties of climate and injury placed heavy demands on the family's day-to-day existence. The high expectations of the family as formal educator simply could not be realized given the economic and social reality of the settlement.

The Puritans increasingly depended upon the school as the basic agency for literacy and a significant means for educating children in the common values and ways of the society. While the schools were not charged solely with the responsibility of catechizing the young, religious values were so much a part of the community that orthodoxy influenced almost all the areas of instruction. For example, *The New England Primer* used verses related to bible stories to illustrate particular letters in the alphabet. The most familiar verse, of course, is the one attached to the letter "A": "In Adam's fall, we sinned all." With the creation of tax-supported schools, dame schools, and the establishment of Harvard College, the Puritans created a configuration of formal instruction at various levels for different segments of the population. While attendance at the schools was often itinerant, and advanced schooling reserved for the affluent, the school in the early colonial period must be seen as an important agency for the education of the New England public.

In addition to the household, church and school, Cremin suggests that we add the invention of the printing press as a fourth element in the educational configuration.[8] The availability of printing presses throughout the colonies provided written materials at a relatively low cost, indirectly increased the rate of literacy and encouraged the possibility of self-education. In colonial America, newspapers, tracts and pamphlets of all sorts informed people of the events and intellectual currents occurring in other communities. Newspapers, in particular, helped develop feelings of interdependence that books imported from abroad could not convey. These various publications cultivated an American vernacular. They encouraged the development of a distinctive language, similar to yet different from the mother tongue of England.

While the Puritan tradition is basic to our language and understanding of the public, I do not want to obscure the pluralistic nature of the American experience in the colonial period. The Puritan attempt to establish a holy commonwealth was one experiment among many others in colonial America. No single colony firmly established a blueprint for America's future. All the colonies, however, shared the basic educational configuration of household, church, school and publications. This configuration shifted in the 17th century as the power of the several agencies was redistributed. The influence of the school and the newspaper grew while that of the household and the church declined. Work outside the home became more prevalent and acted as a mediator of the various influences current in the society. Thus, the power of the church waned while the brokering of merchants and tradespeople increased in importance as the essential influence on public life.

Toward a National Culture

Throughout the shifting rearrangements of these various agencies in the society, however, there persisted a common set of values that were relatively widespread and shared by many colonists as the 1776 War of Independence occurred, the

Constitution was written and the settlement of the western frontier begun. The substance of this *paideia* was established largely by 1) Protestant versions of Christianity, 2) the rational and utilitarian assumptions of the Enlightenment, and 3) the belief that America was a new and providentially established society (literally—as the national seal states—"a new order in society").[9]

1. Throughout the colonial period, American culture was defined by Protestant versions of Christianity. Although Catholics were represented in significant numbers in several of the colonies and Jewish communities were present in a few, the tone of the society was determined by Protestants. This does not mean that most of the colonists attended church, nor that a majority were actually church members; it does suggest, however, that Protestant manners, morals and temperaments determined the ethos of the culture. (One effect of the revivals held during the Great Awakening in the 1740s was the dissemination of Protestant feelings and sensitivities in an intensifed way throughout the colonies.)

2. At the same time that the colonies were defined by the assumption that the culture was Protestant, the culture was being shaped as well through the influence of the rationalistic thought of the Enlightenment. The ideas of John Locke and Isaac Newton were popularized in America through such persons as Benjamin Franklin, Tom Paine and Thomas Jefferson. At the center of the various intellectual movements collectively represented by the term Enlightenment was the notion that the universe operated through predictable laws of cause and effect, that God was essentially a Supreme Being whose identity was more that of a Prime Mover than a personal Saviour, and that government was based upon the mutual interests of individuals whose rights were expressed in a social contract.

3. The third component in the general configuration of values that formed the colonial mind was the belief that America was especially chosen as a promised land. From the Old Testament and from John Locke as well, colonial Americans interpreted the American experience as the latest visitation of Providence. For example, both John Adams and Thomas Jefferson suggested that the national seal should portray "the cloud by day and the pillar by night" that had guided the Israelites through the wilderness. Even Benjamin Franklin maintained that the seal

should draw upon another Hebraic motif—that of Moses dividing the Red Sea in the Exodus.

One factor that augmented the colonists' sense of being a people who shared a destiny was the size of the population. Whether referring to New England villages, Middle Atlantic towns, or Virginia plantation society, the colonies were relatively small units of people who gathered in face-to-face relationships. The body politic in these regional and local communities contained a degree of homogeneity that sustained common cultural ideals and was able to assimilate newcomers into existing patterns of public life over a period of time. In this regard, it is important to remember that the period from 1607 (the settlement in Jamestown) to the Revolution of 1776 constitutes almost half of the actual history of America itself. We tend to begin American history with the Revolution rather than perceiving the Revolution as a midpoint in our history. To speak of the "colonial period" is to refer to over 169 years and several generations of colonists. In collapsing this era into the neat chapters of a school textbook, we tend to lose sight of the complex developments that occurred over many years to sustain an emerging sense of being a distinctive people. While regional and ethnic loyalties remained quite strong, the Revolution of 1776 happened only after some sense of cohesiveness had been built among the different colonies.

After the Revolutionary War, the colonists faced the question of the public more explicitly, how to make one people out of the variety of folk who had once been Virginians, Pennsylvanians or New Englanders. For Thomas Jefferson, one means of educating this diverse public was the creation of a system of schools that could provide basic requirements for literacy and inculcate values common to all the colonies. Schools, therefore, were to make citizens, transmit national values and prepare individuals for participation in the progress of the Republic.

Jefferson made a formal proposal to the Virginia legislature in 1779 for state supported schools. He advocated the establishment of a formal system of education that would include three years of instruction for everybody and advanced schools and colleges for the more intellectually gifted. While his proposal was not accepted by the legislature, his concern for schools was sustained later in the century as local and state agencies were established in various parts of the country to provide for the basic education of the public.

In developing a formal system of public schools, few people in the 19th century expected schools to assume the whole responsibility for education in the society. Not even when common schools were relatively widespread was the school per se expected to be the sole agency of education in the community. Family activities, churches, Sunday Schools, libraries, civic celebrations, service groups, philanthropic societies, apprenticeships, newspapers, tracts and political parties were just a few of the agencies of everyday life that joined in the public's education. The public school, though, grew increasingly in the 19th century to occupy the predominating role in public education as local school districts were created throughout the country to provide free instruction.

Schools for the Public

The most influential spokesman for the emerging common school was the Massachusetts State Secretary of Education, Horace Mann (1796-1859). Although trained as a lawyer, Mann spent most of his life as the leader of the movement to support common schools for educating the American public. Through a series of *Annual Reports*, Mann articulated the fundamental philosophy of education that was presumed in the growing development of free schools across the country. His *Twelve Reports for the Massachusetts State Board of Education* represents a classic argument for free, tax-supported schooling for all children.

While we take a system of public schools for granted, we should not read back into the 19th century our own predisposition. There was not unanimous agreement on this issue. Many people resisted the egalitarian thrust of the common school movement. There was a great deal of protest from the affluent against the idea that the wealthy should be taxed to provide schooling for the poor. The matter was complicated by concern from some churches that the common school would work against sectarian interests. In confronting these various protests against common schools, Mann worked out in his *Annual Reports* the essential form and mission of the American system of public schooling.

In responding to the protest against tax support, Mann reminded his critics of the necessity of an informed electorate in a democratic society. He also warned establishment figures of the dangers that lay in an "uneducated" populace that threatened to undermine the status quo. Mann suggested that common schools led by professional teachers could inculcate support for the American system of free enterprise and respect for the established institutions of the Republic. Mann implied that, educated for citizenship in this way, the potential mob could be controlled.[10]

In regard to the sectarian critique, Mann offered a nondenominational approach to religion in the public schools. He affirmed the religious nature of education, but argued against the cultivation of particular denominational creeds and dogmas. The Massachusetts educator advocated a common set of moral and spiritual values that he felt could best be communicated by the daily reading of the King James version of the Bible and the cultivation of moral character in the regularities of the school itself.[11]

In idealistic terms, Mann argued the case for the right of each individual to have access to education. He spoke eloquently of the virtues of the intellect and the humanizing influence of education on the society.

> Education has never yet been brought to bear with one hundredth part of its potential force, upon the natures of children, and, through them, upon the character of men, and of the race. . . . Here, then, is a new agency, whose powers are just beginning to be understood, and whose mighty energies, hitherto, have been but feebly invoked; and yet, from our experience, limited and imperfect as it is, we do know that, far beyond any other earthly instrumentality, it is comprehensive and decisive . . .[12]

The creation of public schools spurred the development of textbooks that became the basic tools for instruction. While Noah Webster's blue-backed speller had replaced the earlier primer of colonial times as a main text in 18th-century schools, the primary text of the 19th-century public schools was William Holmes McGuffey's series of *Eclectic Readers.* First printed in 1836, the McGuffey *Readers* eventually reached a publication figure of over 100 million copies. Robert Lynn has characterized the *Readers* as an "American civil catechetics," because of the extent to which these readers conveyed basic American values as defined by established institutions and public leaders.[13] Throughout the texts there was explicit concern to build character and to mold individuals in that set of feelings and actions that corresponded with the accepted mores of the culture. The substance of this instruction in the national ethos was composed of several major tenets: 1) a belief in the orderliness of a universe controlled by a benign but distant supreme being, 2) the assumption that progress was the essential characteristic of American history, 3) the acceptance of cultural stereotypes concerning racial and ethnic groups, and 4) the fundamental conviction that right and wrong could be clearly discerned and appropriately rewarded and punished.[14]

The heart of this 19th-century *paideia* was the firm conviction that America was God's noblest experiment and the nation's history was no less than the narrative of Providence's latest experiment with the human race. To be an American was to accept this civil catechism and to adopt the ways and attitudes of those preeminent Americans who occupied the established centers of power and influence. In 19th-century America, the center was occupied by affluent white, Anglo-Saxon Protestants.

Protestants and the Public

Protestant attempts to define America as particularly Christian and especially Protestant have tended to revolve around educational issues. Beginning with the revivals of the Second Great Awakening in the early 19th century, various Protestants have tried to shape the American public within their own particular brand of republicanism. Evangelical efforts to civilize the Mississippi Valley and establish schools, churches and various associations were aimed at sustaining peculiarly Protestant notions of the nature of the Republic. Camp meetings, traveling circuit riders, colporteurs of various tract societies, temperance crusaders, antislavery societies, and associations for the establishment of colleges and academies were just a few of the various reformers and reform efforts financed by Protestants to educate Americans.

Perhaps the most influential component in this collection of educating agencies was the Sunday School that was originally created by lay members of the churches. The Sunday School operated outside official denominational channels, and developed a vast network of teachers, administrators, and shared curricula. In many places, the Sunday School functioned as the only school available for instruction in reading, writing and other basic skills. In this sense, it was a precursor of the common school movement. Later, as this movement spread across the country, many of the church leaders who had been active in the Sunday School became supporters of the free school enterprise as well. What developed out of this cooperative relationship was a dual pattern of partnership between the Sunday School and public school as the key agencies in the basic Protestant strategy for the education of the public. Both schools agreed on a common content of moral education that was communicated broadly through the public schools and interpreted more denominationally on Sunday by the churches. Working together, the churches and the schools anticipated that they could educate the nation in this Protestant *paideia*.

The problem with Protestants is that we have tended to see people different from ourselves as inferior. Education within this context has been understood as a matter of uplifting different groups into the mainstream, or if they could not be uplifted then it was felt that they at least could be trained to know their place. The popular image of the melting pot worked for large numbers of immigrants who could pass over the cultural line and adopt American ways defined by this elite minority. But for those whose color or religion did not permit easy passage, then the ghetto, rather than Main Street, represented for them the American way of life.

Catholics, for example, recognized the Protestant character of the public schools and chose to develop an educational configuration that existed as a counterpoint to the predominating public (Protestant) ones. Thus, Catholic schools, newspapers, hospitals, service and social organizations existed alongside their public counterparts. The most extensive agency, however, was the parochial schools that were established as a result of the Catholic hierarchy's decision to build schools even before churches. State monies were denied Catholics in the creation of these school systems and the parochial school was almost universally regarded by Protestants as essentially anti-American. While some Protestant immigrants created similar institutions, they were largely temporary measures that were usually abandoned as the process of acculturation increased. The strong exception to this tendency is the persisting pattern of parochial schools sponsored by the Missouri Synod Lutheran and Christian

Reformed churches, and the intentional communities of the Amish. The irony, however, in this history of counter-institutions is that in pursuing a separate course, the parochial school has been no less patriotic than the public schools. The Catholic Church has been an American church and its vast networks of organizations have been significant means of permitting Catholics to remain Catholic as they have sought to become Americans.

Jewish immigrants have attended public schools, but many traditional Jews have created their own systems of education in place of the public schools or else have had their children attend both the public school and a religious school at the same time. Those Jewish children who did opt for the public schools had to endure blatant forms of religious discrimination in classrooms that presumed that the Christian faith was the American form of religion. Overt Christian symbols, songs and scripture were often used in classrooms with little concern for the faith and feelings of Jewish children.

19th Century School History from the Bottom Up

Besides the difficulties of Protestants recognizing the diversity of Americans as something to be appreciated rather than overcome, there also existed beneath the rhetoric of public school idealism an underside which contradicted the manifest purposes of free schooling. Neither black nor native-American children were included within the democratic educational vision of Thomas Jefferson and Horace Mann. The children of poor white families, likewise, were often excluded from consideration, or were viewed as objects of charity and targets of reform.

While it is always difficult to ascertain motives, the history of public schooling does reveal a mixture of many different motives. In particular, tension has always been present within the often contradictory purposes of public schooling as a means of social mobility on the one hand and a mode of social control on the other. It is not certain that public schools have had as much respect for individual differences as they have been intent on reforming children within the values of the dominant culture. In this context, schools have sometimes tended to be training grounds for industry and arbitrators of potential social unrest which, if otherwise left unchecked, might have erupted into more radical forms of protest. Indeed, alongside Horace

Mann's appeal for the support of public schools on the grounds of democratic idealism, there exist at the same time within his *Reports* parallel arguments for support which are based on schooling's usefulness as an agency of control and containment. In this light, one can perceive the shape of contemporary educational problems in these tensions which have been present in the history of public schools since their beginning in the early 19th century.

Public schools have been most educationally significant in those places where the culture of the school matched the ethos of the society from which its students originated. Where there has been relatively little diversity in terms of social, economic and ethnic backgrounds, the public schools have been important agencies of nurturing citizens, communicating basic skills and giving encouragement to the individual development of students. It is in those communities, however, where this simultaneity does not exist that tensions have been most noticeably present. I want to deal more specifically with this matter as a contemporary educational problem later in this monograph, but for now it is important at least to mark the fact that tensions were present within the early history of schooling which still remain with us today. No matter how strongly we may want to support the idea of public schools, this support will remain ill founded unless it is aware of the questions which arise from the bottom as well as the top of the social pyramid.[15]

Education and Schooling

By the beginning of the 20th century the combined effects of industrialization, immigration and urbanization upset the more traditional educational patterns that had been based essentially on an agricultural and rural way of life. It was this set of rapidly changing conditions that led John Dewey to devote much of his life and writing to the problem of the public's education. Dewey was uneasy with the capabilities of traditional agencies of education in an industrial age. He felt that much of education was in fact miseducative. It encouraged wrong habits of thinking and did not cultivate skills that were needed to cope with the emerging society. This miseducation threatened the continuation of a democratic society that depended on an educated public. Dewey's solution to this problem was to reconceptualize the nature of the school's role in public education.

Dewey saw the school as an "embryonic society." The school was a miniature version of the public at large. It was in this small public that the habits of inquiry, democratic experience and scientific method could be cultivated and practiced so that they could be exercised at a later time in the society itself. In this way, the schools could address the "problem of the public" that was for Dewey the need for improving "the methods and conditions of debate, discussion and persuasion," necessary for a democratic society.[16] While Dewey did not advocate the expansion of schooling to the point where it became the only agency of public education, it must be recognized that the nature of the school was transformed by Dewey and his enthusiasts in the progressive era. The result of this transformation was the increased monopolization of education by the formal system of schooling and the accompanying growth of the bureaucratic nature of schooling itself.

The result of this history is that we have more and more concentrated educational concerns in the schools and, in turn, have marginalized the significance of other educational agencies in the society. The school has gradually taken on responsibilities formerly shared by several community agencies. We have turned to the schools for acculturation, employment training, moral education and discipline. Thus, the fourfold configuration of school, church, household and publications has tended to shrink in our minds to that of a single agency, the school, whose role, of course, has been proportionately expanded.

In suggesting that education has become almost solely identified with schooling, I do not mean to infer that education is not occurring in the rest of society. What I am maintaining is that as our educational expectations have narrowed to the school, we increasingly do not recognize the educational significance of other agencies in the community.

We will not be able to address adequately the problems of public education until we can recognize the limitations of our tendency to identify public education with public schooling. We need to broaden our perspective to include all those other agencies that together represent the educational systems of our culture. This, of course, is not a new difficulty. As I have tried to suggest in this brief historical survey, ever since the Puritans first turned to schools to supplement the educational responsibilities of family, church and community, Americans have been placing exaggerated expectations on the schools.

What is new, however, is an accumulating series of questions about the nature of education which have been deferred in the development of schools, but which are now so central to the current crisis in schooling and the larger problems of the public that we cannot easily avoid them. In particular, the inherent tension between the school as an equalizer in society and its function as an agency of social control has reached a critical point. The disparity between public schools in rich and poor regions of the country grows more alarming each year. At the same time that these fundamental problems exist, we are in the midst of a change once again in the basic educational configuration that has been caused by the emergence of television as a major educating medium. Finally, we have yet to consider the fundamental nature of knowledge which lies at the center of our educational expectations.

Contemporary Educational Problems

In the current crisis of the public's education, a first step toward possible futures lies in the insistence that schooling issues cannot be adequately assessed unless they are seen within the larger perspective of the problems of education in contemporary society. Within this context, I want to examine four educational problems that lie in the background of current debates about schooling: the school as a certifier of roles in society, the confusing of access to schooling with equal opportunity, the expanding place of television as a primary educator, and the nature of knowledge in the modern world.

Schools and Certification

While schools were previously only one of several different means of becoming adult, establishing roles and finding occupations in society, they have now become, in Thomas Green's words, "very nearly the sole path for gaining access to full-fledged adult membership in American society."[17] Schools have become the primary agency for "certifying, sorting and selecting" what roles persons will occupy in society. Green points to the use of the term "dropout" as symptomatic of the change. Prior to 1950, it was possible for a young person to leave school without completing the 12th grade and not be viewed as a failure. Today, however, dropping out of school bears the onus of leaving society itself. As the school has taken on more of the responsibility for certification, the failure to complete school has therefore changed the school dropout to a dropout from society. Failure in school has become one way in which society has said to many young people that they are simply good for nothing. The deeper impact of this critique is felt in the extent to which manpower training (certification for jobs) has become an essential focus of the public schools. The change is insidious when one considers the quality of the training itself. Indeed, what the schools tend to certify is not so much competency in certain skills as the capacity to take orders, follow instructions and remain relatively docile.[18]

In assigning roles in society, the school more or less confirms cultural stereotypes. If the society is racist and sexist we should hardly expect that we would not find similar perspectives in the classroom. One of the most poignant descriptions of discrimination is Malcolm X's retelling of the day when his high school teacher asked him what he intended to do after graduation. Malcolm replied that he wanted to go on to college and become a lawyer. In response, the teacher said:

> Malcolm, one of life's first needs is to be realistic. . . . You need to think about something you can be. You're good with your hands—making things. . . . Why don't you plan on carpentry?[19]

In the same way, one only has to look through school textbooks to see the extent to which sexual stereotypes determine roles—regardless of the particular gifts, interests and sensitivities of the individual girl or boy. For example, listen to the roles and expectations communicated in an elementary school reader. The following dialogue takes place within a continuing story of a family with two children, a girl named Janet and a boy named Mark. This particular excerpt concerns an incident in which Mark is portrayed as teaching Janet how to skate:

> "Mark! Janet!" said Mother
> "What is going on here?"
>
> "She cannot skate," said Mark.
> "I can help her.

> I want to help her.
> Look at her, Mother.
> Just look at her.
> She is just like a girl.
> She gives up."

Mother forces Janet to try again.

> "Now you see," said Mark.
> "Now you can skate.
> But just with me to help you."[20]

Sexual role stereotyping is a primary educational problem carved literally into the walls of our schools. It is not simply a matter of architectural esthetics that caused schools to have "Boys" and "Girls" etched into the stone above separate entries to many school buildings, but this bit of iconography signified quite explicitly one of the key certifying functions of the school in a society that still attaches rigid expectations according to sex. Moreover, the problem is not only a question of girls and boys being expected to fulfill certain role expectations for it is also a matter of the curriculum itself. Schools assign traditional masculine and feminine character to subjects so that math and science are perceived as hard, tough, masculine areas, whereas subjects like poetry, music and art are seen as soft feminine concerns. In the wider society, those jobs traditionally related to women remain in an inferior status. As women have gained more access to male dominated occupations like law, medicine and business, we have sometimes reinforced the judgment that roles usually identified with women are insignificant. We continue to devalue the nurturing, caring and teaching responsibilities.

An auxiliary agency tied to the school's process of certification is the 20th-century phenomenon of testing. Designed as a means of measuring, objectively, intellectual ability, tests have become powerful filtering devices for deciding who will and who will not be admitted to certain colleges and universities, high school classes and various forms of special education in the elementary schools. For example, while the prestigious Educational Testing Service (ETS) rejects the accusation that the Scholastic Aptitude Test (SAT) presumes to measure intelligence, it does claim that the SAT does assess certain abilities. In regard to the SAT, the ETS officials state: "It is a test of developed ability, not of innate intelligence, a test of abilities that are developed slowly over time both through in-school and out-of-school experience."[21]

The tests, however, are used as if they do measure innate intelligence. They are administered to youth from many different social, economic and cultural backgrounds as if they were all in the same situation. The result is predictable. The affluent are measured to be brightest as well as richest. There is a direct relationship between scores on the Scholastic Aptitude Test and the economic situation of the tested young people. For example, data for 1974 are shown on the following chart:

The Relationship of College Board Scores (SATs) And Family Incomes (1973-74)[22]

Student's Score	Student's Mean Family Income
750—800	$24,124
700—749	21,980
650—699	21,292
600—649	20,330
550—599	19,481
500—549	18,824
450—499	18,122
400—449	17,387
350—399	16,182
300—349	14,355
250—299	11,428
200—249	8,639

As James Loewen, a critic of testing, has suggested: "Tests may measure aptitude or achievement within populations that share backgrounds, but they do not measure accurately across backgrounds." He goes on to add, "If you have two kids who get 500, one from Harvard and one from Tougaloo, you know that one of them is pretty dumb, and it's the one from Harvard."[23]

Testing is another illustration of the limited use of formal schooling in developing a more egalitarian society. The myth has been that schools and universities through selective education could confer legitimacy on the most talented in the society with the poor and less affluent having a chance to become certified for advancement through merit. What we see though is that only a very small fraction of the nonaffluent ever get the same chance as the more affluent. The factor of preselection works over and over again to give unfair advantage to those who by birth are part of the "entitled" class. In his introduction to Richard de Lone's *Small Futures,* which is an analysis of the Carnegie Council on Children study, *All Our Children,* Kenneth Keniston summarizes what this critique implies for the future of reform efforts:

> For well over a century, we Americans have believed that a crucial way to make our society more just was by improving our children. We propose instead that the best way to insure more ample futures for our children is to start with the difficult task of building a more just society.[24]

While this does not permit schools to evade responsibility for the education of the young, neither does it allow the society to foist upon the schools those reforming impulses and idealistic goals that we need to pursue directly in the economic, cultural and political structures of our nation. Part of our difficulty lies in the assumption that the existence of the public school guarantees equality in a democratic society. This assumption itself is another educational problem.

Equal Access and Equal Opportunity

Our society tends to identify access to schooling with equalization of opportunity in the society itself. While schools have enabled many of the poor and disadvantaged to get higher paying jobs than their fathers and mothers, this function of schooling has been less significant than we might have once imagined. In centering almost all of our hopes for a more just society in the school we have deferred other social and governmental possibilities for tax reform, health care and employment.

In educational matters we continue to place the responsibility for success or failure in schooling on the individual child. We sometimes envision schooling as a race where all contenders have an equal opportunity to win. We presume that all the racers come to the starting line having had similar opportunities for training, conditioning and prior practice. A more realistic picture is to imagine schooling as the same race but with contenders who include the lame, the halt and the blind as well as the more recognizable athletes who have two strong legs, adequate nourishment, and professional coaching. Thus seen in this image, the race is grossly unfair. Moreover, one would have to be particularly mindless to suggest that the race itself will do that much to correct the handicaps of the runners. No, in large measure, the race, like the school, simply confirms the pre-race selection.

Hannah Arendt once suggested that the essence of education is natality—the fact that we are born into the world.[25] One of the realities that follows from this observation is that a child has no choice over the circumstance of birth. The accidents of time and place, family, social status and emotional stability are established before birth and there is nothing a child can do to alter these given circumstances. Indeed, much of early childhood development is centered in the ways in which the youngster makes sense out of this given world of the family. Most children are able to accomplish this task relatively unscarred by the peculiarities of their situations, but for many other children the price of making sense is the cost of their own well-being. While affluent families are not spared emotional scarring, the possibility of such pain is increased in families where poverty, poor housing, and unemployment create a set of circumstances that exacerbate the everyday conflicts of life. In poverty, the child carries an extra heavy burden for her or his development.

We so often regard the family as a private world that we tend to ignore the public nature of family life. In talking about children we sometimes suspend our critical awareness of economic and social realities to deal with the individual child as if he or she exists in a vacuum. In reflecting on the nature of the family as educator we too often bypass the harder questions about the social factors that affect the lives of children and youth.

Americans have always had a tendency to avoid dealing with class differences except insofar as we make lower economic classes responsible for overcoming the inequities that have resulted from the affluence of the middle and upper classes of the society. Yet, the question of education cannot be separated from the issue of the nature of the public world that supports, exploits or is benignly indifferent to the needs of our children.

This problem is exacerbated in our time because we have done such a good job of selling schooling as a means of social mobility and increased earning power that we find it difficult now in an era of shrinking economic growth and unemployment to provide a basic and adequate rationale for education itself apart from these utilitarian goals. When education has been trivialized into the notion of schooling as occupational training and role-conditioning, we have lost the genius and the vitality of education. Schooling loses its context. To be more precise, what we have done is sever the connection between schooling and education. In doing so, we have robbed young people of the vital relationship between education and their own development.

If one raises an objection to this characterization of the society and of public schooling, it is important to take into consideration the class context of the objection. The public schools that do enable participation in the public tend to be schools located in relatively affluent areas of the country where the economic and social homogeneity of the population provides a milieu which supports formal schooling. In neighborhoods, towns and cities where poverty, segregated patterns of housing and the decline of community agencies are the facts of life, the schools tend to reflect the critique that has been discussed here. The crisis resides in the increasing numbers of schools that do not function as communities of learning, but rather exist as academies of miseducation. This problem is made even more complex today by the presence of mass media, especially television, which sustain perceptions of the world in a regular and systematic way every day of our lives.

Television—The First Curriculum

Television is a new educative force that is at least as powerful as—if not more persuasive than—any of the conventional modes of instruction now existing in our culture. Neil Postman writes: "Television is not only a curriculum but constitutes the major educational enterprise now being undertaken in the United States. That is why I call it the first curriculum. School is the second."[26]

Television's impact was made clear to me several years ago when I was part of a group that visited an educational experiment called "The Little Red Schoolhouse," which had been created by the Ojibways out of concern for the members of the tribe who had moved from their reservation to St. Paul, Minnesota. Caught in the vicious web of unemployment and poverty, the Ojibway children were often dropouts from the school system. As a means of restoring some sense of identity as Ojibways to their youth, tribal elders had been able to secure an old public school building and to create an independent school, staffed by native teachers, especially for tribal children in the inner city of St. Paul.

The old schoolhouse was transformed by the art, artifacts, and visible cultural symbols of the tribe. The children were conventionally divided into classes, but the usual recreation and arts program had been informed by the heritage of the people themselves. Ojibway dances, songs, and stories fitted naturally and regularly into the daily life of the school. Tribal elders mingled among the children, their parents served as aides, and older youth were in the building working in special programs for the Ojibway community at large.

One morning I was invited to visit a first grade class that was beginning instruction in the native Ojibway language. The leaders of the school felt it crucial that the children develop linguistic ability in the language of their ancestors and see that language not as a dead and ancient tongue, but as a contemporary mode of expression. The teacher asked the children to introduce themselves by telling me their Ojibway name and then the English translation of that name. The names were lovely and the children took great pride in them. I was impressed by the way the school had been able to help the children see the importance of their language and heritage. Finally, though, there was one little boy left to speak his tribal name. He hesitated, but the teacher encouraged him and finally in response to the request to speak his name, the child laughed and responded in a loud voice "The Fonz," which was, of course, the name of a popular television star.

Here in the midst of a unique effort to overcome the inadequacies of a public school system that seemed to eradicate native culture rather than honor it, and here in an agency run by and for Ojibways, the pervasive American mass culture was present in the influence of the television sets that inhabited the children's homes and provided another curriculum beside the one that was so carefully and sensitively sustained in the tribe's school. The general and widespread dissemination of information, news and entertainment to the mass audience of the various television networks must be taken into account in any analysis of the various agencies in our society that present and cultivate attitudes, sensibilities and values.

One of the most cogent considerations of television was offered by E.B. White as early as 1938.

> I believe television is going to be the test of the modern world, and that in this new opportunity to see beyond the range of our vision we shall discover either a new and unbearable disturbance of the general peace or a saving radiance in the sky. We shall stand or fall by television—of that I am quite sure.[27]

White wrote these words shortly after attending one of the early demonstrations of television to the public outside the laboratories. Few people had White's sensitivity to perceive the long-range impact of television on the culture itself. He saw that television was not simply going to be an interesting new device. Instead he was aware of the way in which television might become an extension of our ways of being human, or inhuman.

> Clearly the race today is between loud speaking and soft, between the things that are and the things that seem to be, between the chemist of RCA and the angel of God.[28]

The promise, therefore, is the extent to which television is able to extend our world, to open up areas of human life that have been closed to us, and thereby enlarge our sense of the universe and our ability to be a part of it. The problem, however, is the extent to which television makes our immediate experience seem unreal. We tend to accept television's images with little critical thought about their origins and sponsors. We consume television as a finished product and seldom do we take apart the images we are accepting at face value.

Television sometimes encourages the diminution of our own cultural experience. It exacerbates the tendencies already present in our culture to further devalue the importance of individuals making their own culture. Television is a means whereby we can put off and postpone indefinitely our own involvements in the affairs of art, politics and caring that keep us human. Sometimes, however, I think that critics' vehement rejection of television is in reaction to the lost promise that television several years ago seemed to offer for the revitalization of our cultural life. Marshall McLuhan, in particular, represents a spokesman for some exaggerated claims of television's impact on our lives. McLuhan suggested that television would become a means of establishing a global village where connected to each other by cable we could discover a new world of kinship. The promise has never materialized. What we see is what we get from the kind of society in which we live. The American predilection to turn to techniques and gadgets to fix deeper and more complex problems characterizes our approach to television. Television cannot be more or less than the stuff of our own experience.[29]

It is important, however, that we begin to understand the extent to which consciousness and culture are being formed by television. We have not yet discerned the extent of television's influence on processes of thought, perception and learning, but this is a major item of concern for the immediate future. Part of our difficulty, however, in recognizing the role of television as an educational force lies in our inadequate understanding of knowledge itself.

The Nature of Knowledge

We live in a society where value has been largely measured in terms of quantity, and where reality has been determined by reducing the universe to its individual components. In the modern world, which is essentially a creation of the last 200 years, we have moved steadily toward defining life on the basis of the lowest common denominator. Taking apart, analyzing, reducing life to particles, instincts and causes seemingly explain certain phenomena but leave us with an empty feeling that something is missing in the description. The 20th century began with the high optimism of progressive theories of evolution. It was hoped that an enlightened citizenry could wage a war against ignorance, evil and sloth in order to evoke a modern world characterized by advances in technology and society as well. But this century, which has witnessed dramatic scientific achievements, the expansion of knowledge about the physical universe and the development of mass means of communication, has also been the century of Auschwitz, Hiroshima and Vietnam. At the same time that we have been buoyed up by our increasing mastery of the facts of life, we seem more confused than ever before about its value. We have seen human beings emerge who are, as Peter Abbs aptly suggests, "outwardly knowledgeable, inwardly blind; preoccupied with techniques and not with teleologies;

responsive to the dictates of scientific progress, but not to the imperatives of human culture."[30]

In its root meaning, "education" connotes an experience of leading out, of being opened up, yet more and more education in our society has been defined as the transfer of information. We tend to see knowledge as a product that can be wrapped up and passed around as if it were inert. We have little sense that knowledge is not simply the quantification of data but it is also a set of symbols, beliefs, and ways of knowing that emerge from situations in life, history and circumstance.

Our situation is complicated by a naive sense of objectivity that ignores the subjective nature of knowledge. We have tended to devalue the personal aspects of knowing, indicating that education is concerned primarily with the gathering of facts and the development of scientific methods for discerning truth, either in a biology laboratory or in a humanities class examining a literary text. The irony is that in pursuit of knowledge we have established a world that excludes much of the reality that provides meaning for our lives.

E.F. Schumacher, the economist and philosopher, once told of a visit to Leningrad in which he consulted a sightseeing map to figure out where he was in the city. But Schumacher could not locate himself on the map provided by the Russian tourist bureau. When an interpreter noticed his predicament and offered to help, Schumacher explained that the tourist map did not show some of the churches before which he was standing. The interpreter responded, "We don't show churches on our maps." Schumacher protested that one of the churches did seem to be marked on the map. The interpreter then asserted: "That is a museum. . . . It is only the 'living churches' we don't show."[31]

In reflecting on this experience, Schumacher realized that this was not the first time he had been given a map that did not include things that he could see in front of his own eyes. "All through school and university," Schumacher states, "I had been given maps of life and knowledge on which there was hardly a trace of many of the things that I most cared about and that seemed to me to be of the greatest possible importance to the conduct of my life."[32]

The philosophical map of our time is noteworthy not so much because of what it includes as for what it excludes. As might be anticipated, the important contours on our map are shaped largely by scientific ways of knowing. Facts have taken an inordinate position on the map. Issues related to valuing and to considering areas of reality not easily translated into scientific terminology, nor subject to the application of a scientific method, are eased off the map we regard as reality. We have so developed our capacities to analyze the parts of our lives that we have devalued the experience of seeing life as a whole or viewing our individual lives as anything but particular examples of quantifiable generalizations.

In this regard, I am reminded of the lines in C.S. Lewis' *The Hideous Strength:*

> His education had had the curious effect of making things that he read and wrote more real to him than things he saw. Statistics about agricultural labourers were the substance; any real ditcher, ploughman, or farmer's boy, was the shadow. Though he had never noticed it himself, he had a great reluctance, in his work, ever to use such words as "men," or "women." He preferred to write about "vocational groups," "elements," "classes," and "populations": for, in his own way, he believed as firmly as any mystic in the superior reality of the things that are not seen.[33]

In a real sense, though, the problem is not so much science or the scientific method as it is the difficulty of applying scientific methods to concerns of life that cannot be analyzed or measured in the manner demanded by science. Instead of admitting these limitations, there is a tendency in our popular culture to promote a kind of scientism that encourages an objectivity that pretends to reduce all of life to cause, effect and quantity.

The irony of scientism is that it contradicts the nature of science itself. It turns an exploratory methodology into a creedal statement. Furthermore, it denies that science is bound by any human limitations. Scientism tends to forget that at the heart of universe, as in the minutest particles of organic life, there lies a mystery that does not so much confirm our facts as challenge our assumptions and require our participation in its completion and interpretation.

Since curriculum is the form by which we organize knowledge in the school, then the nature of knowledge must be at the center of curricular matters. The subjects that make up the curriculum, the textbooks adopted by a Board of Education, and the relative value of the various aspects of the school's life are all indicative of the facts, values and skills that we deem important for our children and youth to know. In presuming that education is neutral and that there is some incontrovertible body of knowledge, we have taken for granted the nature of reality conveyed by the schools. In a pluralistic society we must know what we are presuming knowledge to be as the basis of the school's curriculum. In this regard, the essential question is not so much what the common denominator is as how the curriculum represents the diversity of our society's ways of knowing.[34]

The most disastrous consequence of pseudo-scientific conceptions of knowledge is that we do not raise the issues that may point us toward understandings that really do matter. If young people are schooled within a context which systematically avoids the questions that are ultimately significant then we have established a curriculum of despair within the process of education itself. We have developed procedures for analyzing human beings as genus and specie, but we have deemphasized the kinds of learning and forms of knowledge that help us as individuals to find meaning in our lives.

The Churches in the Education of the Public

Protestant churches have only occasionally addressed fundamental educational problems on a wide scale and sustained basis. Instead of questioning the myth of equal opportunity through schooling, we have tended uncritically to herald the school as a center of reform and to neglect other basic social reforms that might truly provide for a more egalitarian society. Rather than challenging racist, sexist and class biased role stereotyping in classrooms, we have generally confirmed conventional views. Neither have we seriously addressed the presence of television as a primary educator, nor have we challenged the society's reductionistic understanding of knowledge. We tend to cultivate a dualistic perspective that permits us to participate in the church under one set of assumptions and participate in the society under another. We have generally settled for a watered down set of moralisms as equivalent with religious concerns in the schools.

Churches and Schools

In retrospect, the public school has influenced the nature of educational strategies in the churches without the churches necessarily having much impact on the nature of public education in the schools. More often than not we have participated in the jingoism of a questionable civil religion in the schools which has been perfunctory and superficial. Pledging allegiance to the flag, saying the Lord's Prayer, and reading a verse of scripture have been the particular elements of formal religious presence in the public schools. When prayer and scripture readings were eliminated as devotional practices, few noticed any substantial difference in the ethos and tone of the schools.

On another level of involvement, the churches' concerns for religion in public schooling have been focused on supplementary programs of instruction such as released time for religious education. Significant attempts have been made to include the study of religion within the school curriculum, but few school systems have actually instituted such programs.

Supreme Court decisions in religion and public education have seen religious questions as divisive and sectarian influences potentially dangerous in public school issues. The Court has relegated churches to the periphery of public consideration. Justice Frankfurter, for example, in the *McCollum* case states:

> The sharp confinement of the public schools to secular education was a recognition of the need of a democratic society to educate its children, insofar as the state undertook to do so, in an atmosphere free from pressures in a realm in which pressures are most resisted and where conflicts are most easily and most bitterly engendered. Designed to serve as perhaps the most powerful agency for promoting cohesion among a heterogeneous democratic people, the public school must keep scrupulously free from entanglement in the strife of sects. (*McCollum* v. *Board of Education* 333 U.S. at 216-17) [35]

In drawing the debate over religion in public schools as the struggle between a sacral or a neutral interpretation of public schooling, the Court has tried to avoid the question of values in a pluralistic society. In dealing with areas of conflict, the Court solved the issue by simply avoiding it. This, of course, does not work because it depends upon the most facile definition of religion as sectarianism. It avoids the more important dimension of religion as pertaining to ultimate concerns and meanings of life. Within this framework, excising the churches and religious questions from public schools disguises even more the truly religious nature of education. In this regard we can understand the characterization of the public school as America's established church because of the way in which schools convey ideologies operating at the deepest levels of human vocation and faith. In various epochs this religious-like substance of valuing has been largely Protestant, then Christian and then vaguely religious. In more recent years, it has been almost fully secular, pragmatic and utilitarian. In this regard a scientific worldview reigns as the operative ideology of the schools. We have fled from the threat of sectarian conflict only to find ourselves now in the arms of a secular sectarianism of nationalism, scientism and empiricism.

In regard to this matter, I think that the churches should affirm the pluralistic nature of public schooling and reject the notions of sacrality and neutrality. Education is not neutral and any attempt to sacralize one particular religious tradition in this diverse society cannot be tolerated. Furthermore, is it not a denial of the American public to suggest that the diversity of our culture cannot be fully present within our most prevalent agency of formal education, namely, public schooling? To pretend that differences do not exist is to communicate a view of life that is dishonest to the core. It takes away the opportunity to develop within the schools the ability of our citizenry to live together as individuals with many different perspectives and expressions of faith, yet as persons who are able to affirm within this pluralism the ultimate value of care for each other.

While no one religious group ought to be able to impose its beliefs and rituals within the schools, our children do need to understand the varieties of religious experience and the importance of religion in the lives of so many of their fellow Americans. Moreover they need to develop abilities to recognize the conflicts and real differences that exist in our society. The schools, with the Court's backing, have chosen to avoid controversy in favor of a facile consensus that is simply wrong at some points and socially coercive at others. In this regard, church leaders on the local and national levels have cooperated in many communities to provide opportunities whereby public debate on schooling issues could take place and the more profound problems of equity and educational excellence could be connected to the immediate issue of busing for court ordered desegregation of schools. In this manner, the churches have been instrumental in helping communities recognize the conflict revolving around schooling issues and see this conflict not simply as a potential source of violence but as a possible beginning point for consideration of crucial public problems.[36]

A point of unfinished business is the question of public funds for the parochial schools. This has been one of the bitterest points of tension between Catholics and Protestants. The question is now made more complex by the presence of many different groups that have begun their own schools. The official government position on this matter has remained unchanged, though various supplementary programs in education have made federal funds available to private and parochial schools. Protestants have been generally against aid to parochial and private schools because they felt that this threatened public schools. To give aid to other schools was seen as inviting division in the society and violating constitutional separation of church and state.

Are we not in a time when this issue needs serious reconsideration? Do not Catholic schools, Protestant parochial schools, private schools of all sorts provide for the education of the public? Can we not perceive the public significance of supporting the educational ventures of the many small communities that collectively form the whole? But, if we do favor state and federal aid for private education, what are the criteria for responsibility to the public that must be a part of any such funding proposals?

Faith and Nurture

The Protestant churches need to consider carefully their vocation as educators in the American public. This means recognizing the extent to which we are currently involved in the education of the public. For example, parish tutoring programs, day care centers, adult education seminars, youth groups, community service projects, social actions, and musical and artistic ventures are all means of public education. In particular, we contribute to the public's education as we are faithful to our own calling in the act of worship and in the development of the church as a community of faith. Our commitment to the pluralistic nature of American society should be the occasion for the deepening of our own distinctive ways of being human. The future calls us to join with other groups in our society to rebuild our public life and help reconstruct our missing communities. The question before us, however, is whether we can do this without presuming that this public will necessarily be Protestant.

In attempting to confront the problem of the public, there is always a temptation to reduce the problem to one of personal feelings and immediate community experience. In so doing we establish small groups as substitutes for public associations. In this case, withdrawal becomes a seductive model. By walling ourselves off from the rest of society, we delude ourselves into believing that we have established a public when all we have accomplished is the creation of another ghetto—either of ideas, race or religion. Contrary to this privatistic alternative is the more incisive possibility suggested by Thomas Green:

> The education of the public requires an image of the solidarity of men in a public sufficient to evoke a social commitment of the suburbanite in the solution of the problems in the city, and a social commitment of the rich to the poor, of the religiously diverse to the service of those who do not share their peculiar history or their uniquely defined community.[37]

The public's education, therefore, largely depends upon our increased consciousness of pluralism and the rights of all citizens to equal access to the public as a forum and a shared responsibility. But the awareness of diversity is tied to a parallel appreciation of the fundamental unity of the human race. Green goes on to remind us:

> What is demanded for the modern education of the public is a symbol of the social commitment so necessary in our day, a vivid image of how it is that we are united in spite of our divisions, a conception of the public that bears the mark of *communitas* in the midst of urban technological society but that at the same time does not involve us in the nostalgic return to the small, spatially limited community of New England or the frontier.[38]

Perhaps, the most important public education question for the church is: How does our understanding of God provide what Green calls "a symbol of social commitment"? How does faith help us recognize the interrelationship of issues of power, justice and love? How does it illuminate, and encourage us to take responsibility for, the conditions of our existence? In answering these questions, we should be aware that the concerns of public education are not extrinsic to Christian education; instead they are deeply entwined within our understanding of the difference the Gospel makes in the shape our lives in society and in the perceptions by which we understand the reality of the world. We should move toward a mode of church life which addresses the problem of the public, explores the issues that lie at the center of social dispute and responds to this inquiry through appropriate action. This means probing the congruity between our faith and our actions. For in the words of Wendell Berry, "The test of faith is consistency—not the fanatic consistency by which one repudiates the influence of knowledge, but rather a consistency between principle and behavior."[39]

A word long associated with faith is nurture, and it is precisely the image of caring and enabling which most adequately expresses our calling as educators in the Republic. Along this line, Berry writes:

> An urban discipline that in good health is closely analogous to healthy agriculture is teaching. Like a good farmer, a good teacher is the trustee of a vital and delicate organism: the life of the mind in his community. The ultimate and defining standard of his discipline is his community's health and intelligence and coherence and endurance. This is a high calling, deserving of a life's work.[40]

As Berry suggests, the vocation of educator involves a life's work; it is not a temporary enthusiasm. There are no easy correctives to issues that are so complicated and so tied to basic conflicts within the whole society. Our task is to understand the wider implications of educational issues and at the same time know that the only way we may begin to address these issues is by confronting them in the places where we live. Thus, we need to bring a combination of commitment and competency to bear on public educational problems and to understand the national and global contexts of the immediate educational issues (i.e., schooling) that we face. However, this seldom happens if individuals are unable to make connections between their personal experience and the structures of society. Within the specialized character of our world it is difficult to discern those relatively free spaces where change can occur, but the most obvious as well as the most neglected space is within our own lives. If we do not begin with ourselves there is little hope that groups of people, organizations and lobbies can make much headway.

> The only real, practical, hope-giving way to remedy the fragmentation that is the disease of the modern spirit is a small and humble way—a way that a government or agency or organization or institution will never think of, though a person may think of it; one must begin in one's own life the private solutions that can only in turn become public solutions.⁴¹

An embodiment of this hope-giving way is the story of Myles Horton and The Highlander Folk School, located near Knoxville, Tennessee, which has existed for over forty years as a source of education and change in the South. Highlander has acted on the premise that people of all sorts and conditions can become responsible for their lives. In 1931, Horton was studying the schools of Denmark when he decided to return to Tennessee and begin what turned out to be a life's work. He wrote to a friend:

> I can't sleep but there are dreams. What you must do is go back. . . . Get a simple place . . . move in . . . you're there . . . the situation is there . . . you start with this and let it grow . . . it will build its own structure and take its own form.⁴²

In its own modest way, Highlander has influenced changes in individuals and society. Over the years, Highlander has been subjected to all sorts of harassment, yet it has survived as a signal of hope in difficult times. Highlander has been involved in the labor struggles of the 1930s, the Civil Rights Movement, and the growing self-determination of the people of the southern Appalachians. It was after participating in a conference at Highlander that Rosa Parks decided one day in Montgomery, Alabama, that she was no longer willing to move to the back of the bus—and the rest is history.

> At Highlander, I found out for the first time in my adult life that this could be a unified society, that there was such a thing as people of differing races and backgrounds meeting together in workshops and living together in peace and harmony. It was a place I was very reluctant to leave. I gained there strength to persevere in my work for freedom, not just for blacks but all oppressed people.⁴³

Highlander still draws people together and provides a context in which dispossessed men and women may take first steps toward reclaiming their roles in the public. It continues to raise questions about the problems that corrode the human spirit and threaten the dignity of human beings.

Finally, I want to reiterate the theme that lies in the background of this monograph, namely that our self develops in relationship to others and realizes itself in the midst of settings we call social. If education is ultimately the process of relating the facts and values of our lives, then the quality of our education is largely determined by the nature of the public life that is our environment. In this context, no greater task exists than the effort of a society to create a set of associations, institutions and events that nurture the lives of its citizens. The Israelites called this configuration a people, the Greeks and Romans understood it as the public. Both of them saw their ideal forms of the public and the people deteriorate into tribalism and nationalism through the pull of self-interest and deceit. The promise of the public, though, is always present, for in the ordinary life that we take for granted there is incarnate the hope of the republic of God. This hope transcends, even while including, all the boundaries and "fences of our nature."[44]

Notes

1. Ross Lockridge, Jr., *Raintree County* (Boston: Houghton Mifflin Co., 1948), p.929, quoted in Sidney E. Mead, *The Nation With the Soul of a Church* (New York: Harper & Row, 1975), p.131.

2. For an accessible collection of essays on this topic, see *Religion and Public Education*, edited by Theodore R. Sizer (New York: Houghton Mifflin Co., 1967) and *Religion in America*, edited by John Cogley (New York: Meridian, 1958). Though dated in some ways, these two volumes still represent thoughtful introductions to the issues.

3. Black Elk, quoted in Wendell Berry, *A Continuous Harmony* (New York: Harcourt Brace Jovanovich, Inc., 1972), p. 85. Used by permission.

4. Quoted in Sidney Mead, *The Old Religion in the Brave New World* (Berkeley: University of California Press, 1977), p. 77.

5. See Werner Jaeger, *Paideia: The Ideals of Greek Culture I*, Trans. By Gilbert Highet (New York: Oxford University Press, 1945), pp. 4-13.

6. Lawrence A. Cremin, *Traditions of American Education* (New York: Basic Books, 1976), p. 12. Used by permission. See also Cremin's *American Education: The Colonial Experience* (New York: Harper & Row, 1970) and Bernard Bailyn's *Education in the Forming of American Society* (Chapel Hill: University of North Carolina Press, 1960).

7. John Winthrop, "A Model of Christian Charity," *American Christianity I*, edited by H. Shelton Smith, Robert T. Handy and Lefferts A. Loetscher (New York: Charles Scribner's Sons, 1960), p. 102.

8. Cremin, p. 12.

9. *Ibid.*, p. 87.

10. Horace Mann, "Twelfth Annual Report (1848)," *The Republic and the School*, edited by Lawrence A. Cremin (New York: Teachers College Press, 1957), pp. 86-87.

11. *Ibid.*, pp. 79-112.

12. *Ibid.*, p. 101.

13. Robert W. Lynn, "Civil Catechetics in Mid-Victorian America: Some Notes About American Civil Religion, Past and Present," *Religious Education*, CXVIII (Jan.-Feb. 1973), pp. 5-27.

14. Ruth Miller Elson, *Guardians of American Tradition: American Schoolbooks of the Nineteenth Century* (Lincoln: University of Nebraska Press, 1964), pp. 285,337. For a contemporary analysis, see Frances Fitzgerald, *America Revised* (Boston: Atlantic-Little Brown, 1979).

15. In recent years an impressive number of books and essays have dealt with the underside of American educational history. In particular, I would suggest: Michael B. Katz, *Class, Bureaucracy, and Schools: The Illusion of Educational Change* (New York: Praeger, 1971) and *The Irony of Early School Reform: Educational Innovation in Mid-Nineteenth Century Massachusetts* (Boston: Beacon Press, 1968).

16. John Dewey, *The Public and Its Problems* (Chicago: Swallow Press, 1927), p. 208. See also Dewey's *Democracy and Education* (New York: Free Press, 1916) and Lawrence A. Cremin's interpretative study *The Transformation of the School* (New York: Vintage Books, Random House, Inc., 1964).

17. Thomas F. Green, "Citizenship or Certification," *Anthropological Perspectives on Education*, edited by Murray L. Wise (New York: Basic Books, 1971), p. 133. Used by permission.

18. *Ibid.*, p. 133-135.

19. Malcolm X, *The Autobiography of Malcolm X* (New York: Ballantine Books, Random House, Inc., 1964), p. 36. Used by permission.

20. Quoted by Virginia Kidd in *Demystifying Schools*, edited by Miriam Wasserman (New York: Praeger, 1974), pp. 139-140.

21. Quoted in James Fellows, "The Tests and the 'Brightest': How Fair Are the College Boards," *Atlantic* (February 1980), p. 43.

22. Quoted in Richard de Lone, *Small Futures* (New York: Harcourt Brace Jovanovich, Inc., 1979), p. 102.

23. James Loewen, quoted in "The Tests and the 'Brightest,'" p. 47.

24. Richard H. de Lone, *Small Futures* (New York: Harcourt Brace Jovanovich, Inc., 1979), iv.

25. Hannah Arendt, *Between Past and Future: Eight Exercises in Political Thought* (New York: Viking Press, 1968), p. 174.

26. Neil Postman, "The First Curriculum: Comparing School and Television," *Phi Delta Kappan* (November, 1979), p. 163.

27. Specified excerpt from pp. 2 and 3 in *One Man's Meat* by E.B. White, copyright 1938, 1966 by E.B. White. Reprinted by permission of Harper & Row, Publishers, Inc.

28. *Ibid.*, p. 3.

29. See Marshall McLuhan, *Understanding Media: The Extensions of Man* (New York: McGraw-Hill, 1973).

30. Quoted in Douglas Sloan, "Education and Values," *Teachers College Record*, Vol. 80, no. 3 (February 1979), p. 401.

31. E. F. Schumacher, *A Guide For the Perplexed* (New York: Harper & Row Publishers, 1977), p. 1. Used by permission.

32. *Ibid.*

33. C. S. Lewis, *The Hideous Strength* (New York: Macmillan, 1964), p. 87, quoted in Wendell Berry's *The Unsettling of America* (San Francisco: Sierra Club Books, 1977), p. 142. Used by permission.

34. "Ways of Knowing" is a phrase identified especially with Professor Philip Phenix's work as a teacher and scholar.

35. Quoted by Nicholas Wolterstorff in *Religion and the Schools* (Grand Rapids: Eerdmans, 1966), p. 24. This monograph is a critical analysis of the relationship

between churches and public schools which I have found useful in preparing my own discussion of the topic.

36. See *The Role of the Community in the School Desegregation/Integration Process*, collected and compiled by The National Center for Quality Integrated Education (Valley Forge, Pa.: Ministries in Public Education, 1977).

37. Green, "Citizenship or Certification," p. 142. See also, Lawrence A. Cremin, *Public Education* (New York: Basic Books, 1976) and especially William Greenbaum, "America in Search of a New Ideal: An Essay on the Rise of Pluralism," *Harvard Educational Review*, Vol. 44, No. 3 (August, 1974), pp. 411-440.

38. *Ibid.*

39. Wendell Berry, *A Continuous Harmony*, p. 157.

40. *Ibid.*, p. 135.

41. Wendell Berry, *The Unsettling of America*, p.23.

42. Quoted by Frank Adams in *Unearthing Seeds of Fire: The Idea of Highlander* (Winston-Salem, North Carolina: John F. Blair, Publisher, 1975), p. 24.

43. *Ibid.*, p. 122.

44. James Agee, "Dedication," *The Collected Poems of James Agee*, edited by Robert Fitzgerald (Boston: Houghton Mifflin, 1968), p. 15.

The Education of the Public and the Public School

A Monograph Series of the
UNITED CHURCH BOARD FOR HOMELAND MINISTRIES

Howard E. Spragg, Executive Vice-President

Verlyn L. Barker, Editor
Audrey Miller, Managing Editor
Douglas Sloan, Consulting Editor

The Education of the Public, Malcolm L. Warford

The Anti-Muffins, Madeleine L'Engle

The Public School and the Challenge of Ethnic Pluralism, Carl A. Grant, Marilynne Boyle and Christine E. Sleeter

The Public School and the Education of the Whole Person, Mary Caroline Richards

The Public School and the Family, Hope Jensen Leichter

The Public School and Finances, Mary Frase Williams

The Public School and Moral Education, Henry C. Johnson, Jr.

The Public School and Public Policy, Manfred Stanley

Study/Action Guide for Congregations, Nancy and Manford Wright-Saunders

THE EDUCATION OF THE PUBLIC AND THE PUBLIC SCHOOL

Author: Malcolm L. Warford, **Ed.D.**, Professor of Religion and Education, and Advisor to the President and Board of Directors, Union Theological Seminary, New York, N.Y.; Adjunct Professor, Teachers College, Columbia University. Prior to this present position, he was on the faculty of the Divinity School and College of Arts and Sciences, Saint Louis University and held pastorates in Vermont and New York. He is a trustee of the Maryknoll School of Theology and author of *THE NECESSARY ILLUSION* and numerous articles on education. He is an ordained minister of the United Church of Christ.

To speak of the education of the public is to direct attention to the various means by which a people sustain their common values, beliefs, and behaviors. Within this context, our identification of public education with schooling alone is an indiscriminate use of the terms. They are not the same. Schooling is only one agency in the configuration of agencies that collectively educate the public. Families, political parties, television networks, museums, the armed services, social clubs, and voluntary associations of all kinds together participate in the education of the attitudes and perceptions that shape our private hopes and our public expectations. All of these various agencies should help inform us of our ties to one another, the rest of the world and our place in it. In the current crisis of the public's education, a first step toward possible futures lies in the insistence that schooling issues cannot be adequately assessed unless they are seen within the larger perspective of the problems of education in contemporary society...If education is ultimately the process of relating the facts and values of our lives, then the quality of our education is largely determined by the nature of the public life that is our environment.

The Pilgrim Press
132 West 31 Street
New York, New York 10001

ISBN-0-8298-0418-8 $2.95